PIANO SOLO

TALES OF SOLACE

ISBN 978-1-70512-237-2

Visit Hal Leonard Online at
www.halleonard.com

Contact us:
Hal Leonard
7777 West Bluemound Road
Milwaukee, WI 53213
Email: info@halleonard.com

In Europe, contact:
Hal Leonard Europe Limited
42 Wigmore Street
Marylebone, London, W1U 2RN
Email: info@halleonardeurope.com

In Australia, contact:
Hal Leonard Australia Pty. Ltd.
4 Lentara Court
Cheltenham, Victoria, 3192 Australia
Email: info@halleonard.com.au

IL ÉTAIT UNE FOIS

By STEPHAN MOCCIO

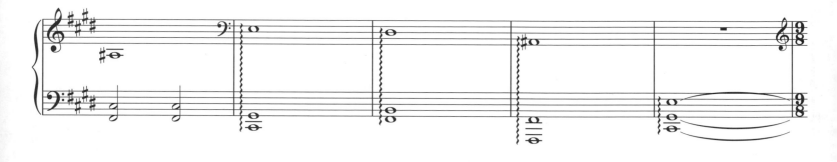

rit. poco a poco

a tempo

FRACTURE

By STEPHAN MOCCIO

Moderately, with freedom and a fragile heart

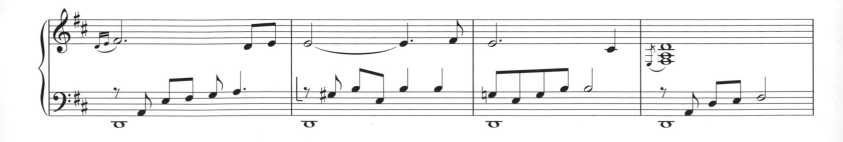

8vb

THIRTEEN

By STEPHAN MOCCIO

Slowly, expressively, with intention

WHITBY

Somewhere by the sea in northern England where the legend of Dracula lives...

By STEPHAN MOCCIO

With motion and passion

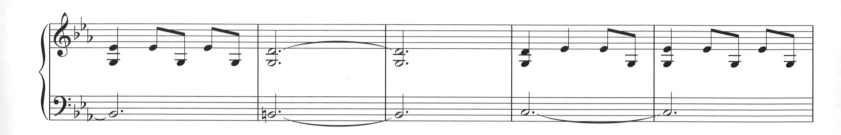

SEA CHANGE

By STEPHAN MOCCIO

LUMIÈRE

By STEPHAN MOCCIO

Désir plein d'espoir

NOSTALGIA

By STEPHAN MOCCIO

With a longing for the past

NUIT BLANCHE

By STEPHAN MOCCIO

THROUGH OSCAR'S EYES

By STEPHAN MOCCIO

With the spirit of wonder and innocence

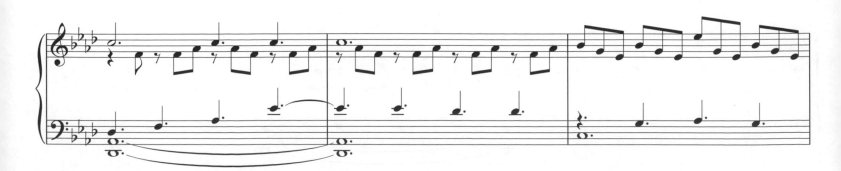

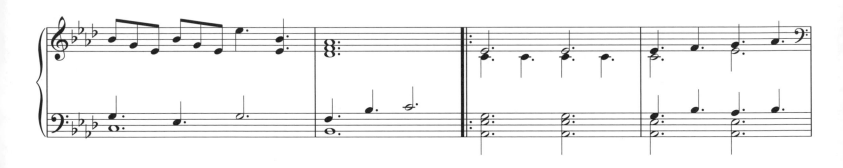

Slowly and freely

LE TEMPS QUI PASSE

By STEPHAN MOCCIO

Modérément, concentrée et précise comme une horloge

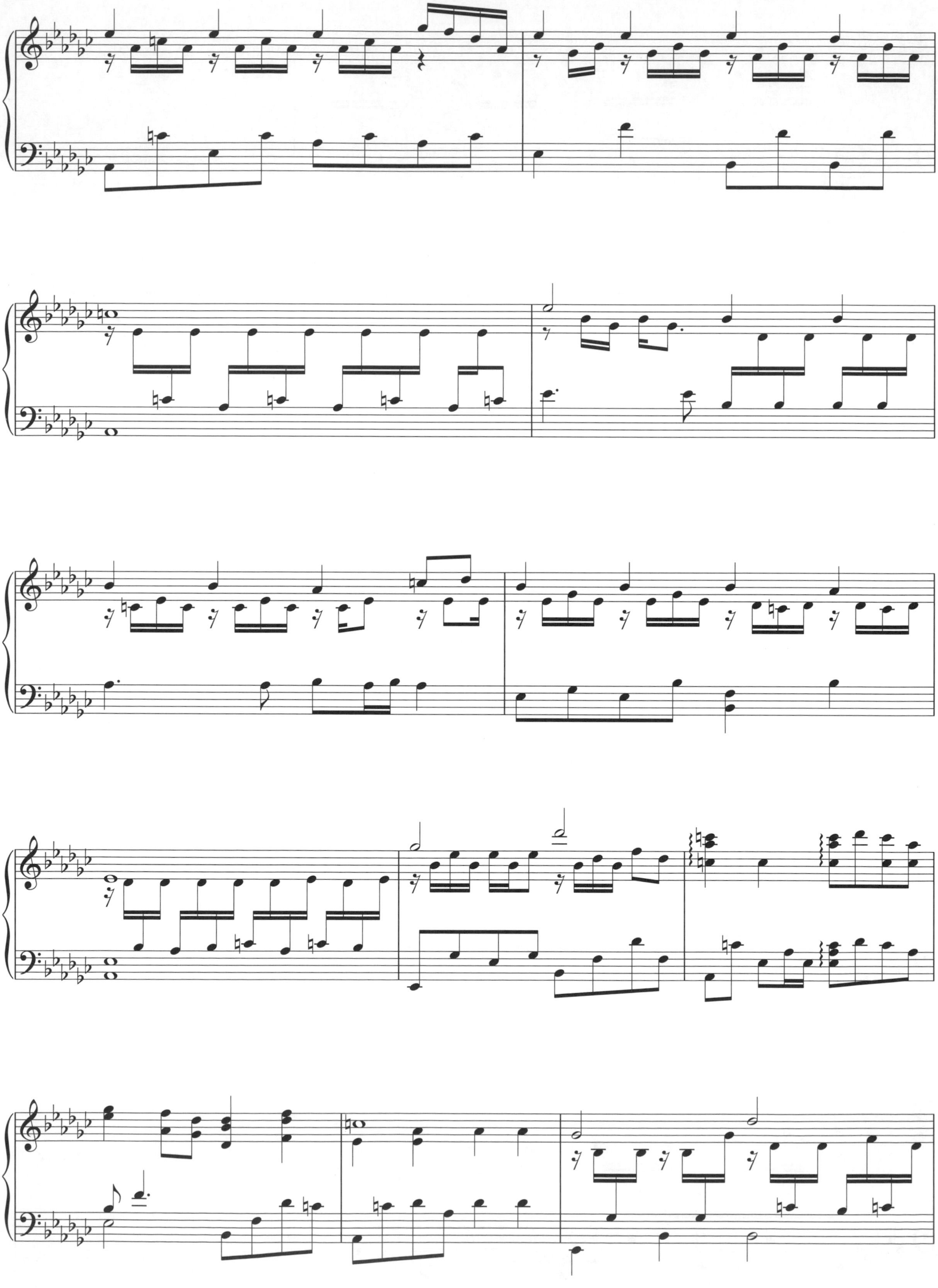

TU ME MANQUES

By STEPHAN MOCCIO

Réfléchissant, avec une certaine nostalgie

SOLACE

By STEPHAN MOCCIO

GHOSTS

By STEPHAN MOCCIO

BURGUNDY

By STEPHAN MOCCIO

FREDDIE'S THEME

By STEPHAN MOCCIO

Moderately slow, expressively and melancholic

LA FILLE AUX POUVOIRS MAGIQUES

By STEPHAN MOCCIO

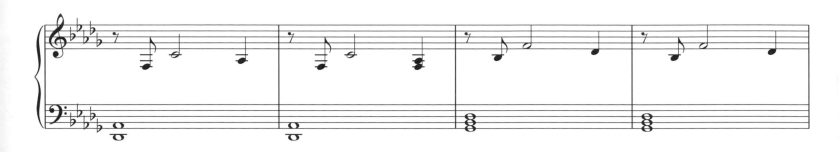